Of Holy Virginity

Of Holy Virginity

St. Augustine

Of Holy Virginity
© Lighthouse Publishing 2018

Written by: St. Augustine (Nov.13 354 – Aug.28 430)

Translated by: Rev. C. L. Cornish. M.A.

Updated into Modern U.S English by A.M. Overett (b. 1960)

All rights reserved. Without limiting the rights under copyright reserved above, no part of this publication may be reproduced, stored in a retrieval system, or transmitted, in any form or by any means (electronic, mechanical, photocopying, recording or otherwise), without the prior written permission of the copyright owner of this book.

Published by
Lighthouse Christian Publishing
SAN 257-4330
5531 Dufferin Drive
Savage, Minnesota, 55378
United States of America

www.lighthousechristianpublishing.com

Introductory Notice.

Retr. ii. 23. "After I had written 'on the Good of Marriage,' it was expected that I should write on Holy Virginity; and I did not delay doing so: and that it is God's gift, and how great a gift, and with what humility to be guarded, so far as I was able I set forth in one volume. This book begins," &c.

1. We lately put forth a book "of the Good of Marriage," in which also we admonished and admonish the virgins of Christ, not, on account of that greater gift which they have received, to despise, in comparison of themselves, the fathers and mothers of the People of God; and not to think those men, (whom the Apostle sets forth as the olive, that the engrafted wild olive be not proud,) who did service to Christ about to come hereafter, even by the begetting of sons, on this account of less desert, because by divine right continence is preferred to wedded life, and pious virginity to marriage. Forsooth in them were being prepared and brought forth future things, which now we see fulfilled in a marvelous and effectual manner, whose married life also was prophetic: whence, not after the wonted custom of human wishes and joys, but by the very deep counsel of God, in certain of them fruitfulness obtained to be honored, in certain also barrenness to be made fruitful. But now, towards them unto whom it is said, "if they contain not, let them be married," we must use not consolation, but exhortation. But them, unto whom it is said, "Whoso can receive, let him receive," we must exhort, that they be not alarmed; and alarm that they be not lifted up. Wherefore virginity is not only to be set forth, that it may be loved, but also to be admonished, that it be not puffed up.

2. This we have undertaken in our present discourse: may Christ help us, the Son of a virgin, and the Spouse of virgins, born after the flesh of a virgin womb, and wedded after the Spirit in virgin marriage. Whereas, therefore, the whole Church itself is a virgin espoused unto one Husband Christ, as the Apostle saith, of how great honor are its members worthy, who guard this even

in the flesh itself, which the whole Church guards in the faith? which imitates the mother of her husband, and her Lord. For the Church also is both a mother and a virgin. For whose virgin purity consult we for, if she is not a virgin? or whose children address we, if she is not a mother? Mary bare the Head of This Body after the flesh, the Church bears the members of that Body after the Spirit. In both virginity hinders not fruitfulness: in both fruitfulness takes not away virginity. Wherefore, whereas the whole Church is holy both in body and spirit, and yet the whole is not virgin in body but in spirit; how much more holy is it in these members, wherein it is virgin both in body and spirit?

3. It is written in the Gospel, of the mother and brethren of Christ, that is, His kindred after the flesh, that, when word had been brought to Him, and they were standing without, because they could not come to Him by reason of the crowd, He made answer, "Who is My mother? or who are My brethren? and stretching forth His Hand over His disciples, He saith, These are My brethren: and whosoever shall have done the will of My Father, that man is to Me brother, and mother, and sister." What else teaching us, than to prefer to kindred after the flesh, our descent after the Spirit: and that men are not blessed for this reason, that they are united by nearness of flesh unto just and holy men, but that, by obeying and following, they cleave unto their doctrine and conduct. Therefore Mary is more blessed in receiving the faith of Christ, than in conceiving the flesh of Christ. For to a certain one who said, "Blessed is the womb, which bare Thee," He Himself made answer, "Yea, rather, blessed are they who hear the Word of God, and keep it." Lastly, to His

brethren, that is, His kindred after the flesh, who believed not in Him, what profit was there in that being of kin? Thus also her nearness as a Mother would have been of no profit to Mary, had she not borne Christ in her heart after a more blessed manner than in her flesh.

4. Her virginity also itself was on this account more pleasing and accepted, in that it was not that Christ being conceived in her, rescued it beforehand from a husband who would violate it, Himself to preserve it; but, before He was conceived, chose it, already dedicated to God, as that from which to be born. This is shown by the words which Mary spoke in answer to the Angel announcing to her her conception; "How," saith she, "shall this be, seeing I know not a man?" Which assuredly she would not say, unless she had before vowed herself unto God as a virgin. But, because the habits of the Israelites as yet refused this, she was espoused to a just man, who would not take from her by violence, but rather guard against violent persons, what she had already vowed. Although, even if she had said this only, "How shall this take place?" and had not added, "seeing I know not a man," certainly she would not have asked, how, being a female, she should give birth to her promised Son, if she had married with purpose of sexual intercourse. She might have been bidden also to continue a virgin, that in her by fitting miracle the Son of God should receive the form of a servant, but, being to be a pattern to holy virgins, lest it should be thought that she alone needed to be a virgin, who had obtained to conceive a child even without sexual intercourse, she dedicated her virginity to God, when as yet she knew not what she should conceive, in order that the imitation of a heavenly life in an earthly

and mortal body should take place of vow, not of command; through love of choosing, not through necessity of doing service. Thus Christ by being born of a virgin, who, before she knew Who was to be born of her, had determined to continue a virgin, chose rather to approve, than to command, holy virginity. And thus, even in the female herself, in whom He took the form of a servant, He willed that virginity should be free.

5. There is, therefore, no reason why the virgins of God be sad, because themselves also cannot, keeping their virginity, be mothers of the flesh. For Him alone could virginity give birth to with fitting propriety, Who in His Birth could have no peer. However, That Birth of the Holy Virgin is the ornament of all holy virgins; and themselves together with Mary are mothers of Christ, if they do the will of His Father. For Mary, also is on this account the Mother of Christ in a way fuller of praise and blessing, according to His sentence mentioned above. "Whosoever doeth the will of my Father Who is in heaven, that one is to Me brother, and sister, and mother." All these degrees of nearness of kin to Himself, He shows forth in a spiritual manner, in the People whom He hath redeemed: as brothers and sisters He hath holy men and holy women, forasmuch as they all are co-heirs in the heavenly inheritance. His mother is the whole Church, because she herself assuredly gives birth to His members, that is, His faithful ones. Also His mother is every pious soul, doing the will of His Father with most fruitful charity, in them of whom it travailed, until Himself be formed in them. Mary, therefore, doing the will of God, after the flesh, is only the mother of Christ, but after the Spirit she is both His sister and mother.

6. And on this account, that one female, not only in the Spirit, but also in the flesh, is both a mother and a virgin. And a mother indeed in the Spirit, not of our Head, Which is the Savior Himself, of Whom rather she was born after the Spirit: forasmuch as all, who have believed in Him, among whom is herself also, are rightly called "children of the Bridegroom:" but clearly the mother of His members, which are we: in that she wrought together by charity, that faithful ones should be born in the Church, who are members of That Head: but in the flesh, the mother of the Head Himself. For it behooved that our Head, on account of a notable miracle, should be born after the flesh of a virgin, that He might thereby signify that His members would be born after the Spirit, of the Church a virgin: therefore Mary alone both in Spirit and in flesh is a mother and a virgin: both the mother of Christ, and a virgin of Christ; but the Church, in the Saints who shall possess the kingdom of God, in the Spirit indeed is altogether the mother of Christ, altogether a virgin of Christ: but in the flesh not altogether, but in certain a virgin of Christ, in certain a mother, but not of Christ. Forsooth both faithful women who are married, and virgins dedicated to God, by holy manners, and charity out of a pure heart, and good conscience, and faith unfeigned, because they do the will of the Father, are after a spiritual sense mothers of Christ. But they who in married life give birth to (children) after the flesh, give birth not to Christ, but to Adam, and therefore run, that their offspring having been dyed in His Sacraments, may become members of Christ, forasmuch as they know what they have given birth to.

7. I have said this, lest haply married fruitfulness dare to vie with virgin chastity, and to set forth Mary herself, and to say unto the virgins of God, She had in her flesh two things worthy of honor, virginity and fruitfulness; inasmuch as she both continued a virgin, and bore: this happiness, since we could not both have the whole, we have divided, that ye be virgins, we be mothers: for what is wanting to you in children, let your virginity, that hath been preserved, be a consolation: for us, let the gain of children make up for our lost virginity. This speech of faithful women married, unto holy virgins, would anyhow be to be endured, if they gave birth to Christians in the flesh; that in this alone, save virginity, the fruitfulness of Mary in the flesh should be more excellent, that she gave birth to the Head Himself of these members, but they to the members of That Head: but now, although by this speech there vie such as on this one account wed and have intercourse with husbands, that they may have sons, and have no other thought of their sons, than to gain them for Christ, and do this so soon as they can: yet are not Christians born of their flesh, but made so afterwards: the Church giving them birth, through this, that in a spiritual manner she is the mother of the members of Christ, of Whom also after a spiritual manner she is the virgin. And unto this holy birth mothers also who have not borne in the flesh Christians, are workers together, that they may become what they know that they could not give birth to in the flesh: yet are they workers together through this, wherein themselves also are virgins and mothers of Christ, that is to say, in "faith which worketh through love."

8. Therefore no fruitfulness of the flesh can be compared to holy virginity even of the flesh. For neither is itself also honored because it is virginity, but because it hath been dedicated to God, and, although it be kept in the flesh, yet is it kept by religion and devotion of the Spirit. And by this means even virginity of body is spiritual, which continence of piety vows and keeps. For, even as no one makes an immodest use of the body, unless the sin have been before conceived in the spirit, so no one keeps modesty in the body, unless chastity have been before implanted in the spirit. But, further, if modesty of married life, although it be guarded in the flesh, is yet attributed to the soul, not to the flesh, under the rule and guidance of which, the flesh itself hath no intercourse with any beside its own proper estate of marriage; how much more, and with how much greater honor, are we to reckon among the goods of the soul that continence, whereby the virgin purity of the flesh is vowed, consecrated, and kept, for the Creator Himself of the soul and flesh.

9. Wherefore neither are we to believe that their fruitfulness of the flesh, who at this time seek in marriage nothing else save children, to make over unto Christ, can be set against the loss of virginity. Forsooth, in former times, unto Christ about to come after the flesh, the race itself of the flesh was needful, in a certain large and prophetic nation: but now, when from out every race of men, and from out all nations, members of Christ may be gathered unto the People of God, and City of the kingdom of heaven, whoso can receive sacred virginity, let him receive it; and let her only, who contains not, be married. For what, if any rich woman were to expend much money on this good work, and to buy, from out different nations,

slaves to make Christians, will she not provide for the giving birth to members of Christ in a manner richer, and more numerous, than by any, how great so ever, fruitfulness of the womb? And yet she will not therefore dare to compare her money to the offering of holy virginity. But if for the sake of making such as shall be born Christians, fruitfulness of the flesh shall with just reason be set against the loss of chastity, this matter will be more fruitful, if virginity be lost at a great price of money, whereby many more children may be purchased to be made Christians, than could be born from the womb, however fruitful, of a single person. But, if it be extreme folly to say this, let the faithful women that are married possess their own good, of which we have treated, so far as seemed fit, in another volume; and let them more highly honor, even as they are most rightly used to do, in the sacred virgins, their better good, of which we are treating in our present discourse.

10. For not even herein ought such as are married to compare themselves with the deserts of the continent, in that of them virgins are born: for this is not a good of marriage, but of nature: which was so ordered of God, as that of every sexual intercourse whatever of the two sexes of human kind, whether in due order and honest, or base and unlawful, there is born no female save a virgin, yet is none born a sacred virgin: so it is brought to pass that a virgin is born even of fornication, but a sacred virgin not even of marriage.

11. Nor do we ourselves set forth this in virgins, that they are virgins; but that they are virgins dedicated unto God by pious continence. For it is not at a venture

that I may say, a married woman seems to me happier than a virgin about to be married: for the one hath what the other as yet desires, especially if she be not yet even the betrothed of any one. The one studies to please one, unto whom she hath been given; the other many, in doubt unto whom she is to be given: by this one thing she guards modesty of thought from the crowd, that she is seeking, not an adulterer, but a husband, in the crowd. Therefore that virgin is with good reason set before a married woman, who neither sets herself forth for the multitude to love, whereas she seeks from out the multitude the love of one; nor, having now found him, orders herself for one, taking thought of the things of the world, "how to please her husband;" but hath so loved "Him of fair beauty above the sons of men," as that, because she could not, even as Mary, conceive Him in her flesh, she hath kept her flesh also virgin for Him conceived in her heart. This kind of virgins no fruitfulness of the body hath given birth to: this is no progeny of flesh and blood. If of these the mother be sought for, it is the Church. None bears sacred virgins save a sacred virgin, she who hath been espoused to be presented chaste unto one Husband, Christ. Of her, not altogether in body, but altogether in spirit virgin, are born holy virgins both in body and in spirit.

12. Let marriages possess their own good, not that they beget sons, but that honestly, that lawfully, that modestly, that in a spirit of fellowship they beget them, and educate them, after they have been begotten, with cooperation, with wholesome teaching, and earnest purpose: in that they keep the faith of the couch one with another; in that they violate not the sacrament of wedlock.

All these, however, are offices of human duty: but virginal chastity and freedom through pious continence from all sexual intercourse is the portion of Angels, and a practice, in corruptible flesh, of perpetual incorruption. To this let all fruitfulness of the flesh yield, all chastity of married life; the one is not in (man's) power, the other is not in eternity; free choice hath not fruitfulness of the flesh, heaven hath not chastity of married life. Assuredly they will have something great beyond others in that common immortality, who have something already not of the flesh in the flesh.

13. Whence they are marvelously void of wisdom, who think that the good of this continence is not necessary for the sake of the kingdom of heaven, but for the sake of the present world: in that, forsooth, married persons are strained different ways by earthly cares more and more straitened, from which trouble virgins and continent persons are free: as though on this account only it were better not to be married, that the straits of this present time may be escaped, not that it is of any profit unto a future life. And, that they may not seem to have put forth this vain opinion from out the vanity of their own heart, they take the Apostle to witness, where he saith, "But concerning virgins I have not command of the Lord, but I give counsel, as having obtained mercy from God to be faithful. Therefore, I think that this is good on account of the present necessity, because it is good for a man so to be." Lo, say they, where the Apostle shows "that this is good on account of the present necessity," not on account of the future eternity. As though the Apostle would have regard for the present necessity, otherwise than as providing and consulting for the future; whereas all his

dealing calls not save unto life eternal.

14. It is, therefore, the present necessity that we are to avoid, but yet such as is a hindrance to somewhat of the good things to come; by which necessity the married life is forced to have thought of the things of the world, how to please, the husband the wife or the wife the husband. Not that these separate from the kingdom of God, as there are sins, which are restrained by command, not by counsel, on this account, because it is matter of condemnation not to obey the Lord when He commands: but that, which, within the kingdom of God itself, might be more largely possessed, if there were larger thoughts how they were to please God, will assuredly be less, when as this very thing is less thought of by necessity of marriage. Therefore he says, "Concerning virgins I have not command of the Lord." For whosoever obeys not a command, is guilty and liable for punishment. Wherefore, because it is not sin to marry a wife or to be married, (but if it were a sin, it would be forbidden by a "Command,") on this account there is no "Command" of the Lord concerning virgins. But since, after we have shunned or had forgiveness of sins, we must approach eternal life, wherein is a certain or more excellent glory, to be assigned not unto all who shall live forever, but unto certain there; in order to obtain which it is not enough to have been set free from sins, unless there be vowed unto Him, Who sets us free, something, which it is no matter of fault not to have vowed, but matter of praise to have vowed and performed; he saith, "I give counsel, as having obtained mercy from God that I should be faithful." For neither ought I to grudge faithful counsel, who not by my own merits, but by the mercy of God, am faithful. "I think

therefore that this is good, by reason of the present necessity." This, saith he, on which I have not command of the Lord, but give counsel, that is concerning virgins, I think to be good by reason of the present necessity. For I know what the necessity of the present time, unto which marriages serve, compels, that the things of God be less thought of than is enough for the obtaining that glory, which shall not be of all, although they abide in eternal life and salvation: "For star differed from star in brightness; so also the Resurrection of the dead. It is," therefore, "good for a man so to be."

15. After that the same Apostle adds, and says, "Thou art bound to a wife, seek not loosening: thou art loosed from a wife, seek not a wife." Of these two, that, which be set first, pertains unto command, against which it is not lawful to do. For it is not lawful to put away a wife, save because of fornication, as the Lord Himself saith in the Gospel. But that, which he added, "Thou art loosed from a wife, seek not a wife," is a sentence of counsel, not of command; therefore it is lawful to do, but it is better not to do. Lastly, he added straightway, "Both if thou shalt have taken a wife, thou hast not sinned; and, if a virgin shall have been married, she sinned not." But, after that former saying of his, "Thou art bound to a wife, seek not loosening," he added not, did he, "And if thou shalt have loosed, thou hast not sinned?" For he had already said above, "But to these, who are in marriage, I command, not I, but the Lord, that the wife depart not from her husband: but, if she shall have departed, that she remain unmarried, or be reconciled unto her own husband;" for it may come to pass that she depart, not through any fault of her own, but of her husband. Then he

saith, "And let not the man put away his wife," which, nevertheless, he set down of command of the Lord: nor did he then add, And, if he shall have put her away, he sinned not. For this is a command, not to obey which is sin: not a counsel, which if you shall be unwilling to use, you will obtain less good, not do any ill. On this account, after he had said, "Thou art loosed from a wife, seek not a wife;" because he was not giving command, in order that there be not evil done, but was giving counsel, in order that there be done what is better: straightway he added, "Both, if thou shall have taken a wife, thou hast not sinned; and, if a virgin shall have been married, she sinned not."

16. Yet he added, "But such shall have tribulation of the flesh, but I spare you:" in this manner exhorting unto virginity, and continual continence, so as some little to alarm also from marriage, with all modesty, not as from a matter evil and unlawful, but as from one burdensome and troublesome. For it is one thing to incur dishonor of the flesh, and another to have tribulation of the flesh: the one is matter of crime to do, the other of labor to suffer, which for the most part men refuse not even for the most honorable duties. But for the having of marriage, now at this time, wherein there is no service done unto Christ about to come through descent of flesh by the begetting of the family itself, to take upon one to bear that tribulation of the flesh, which the Apostle foretells to such as shall be married, would be extremely foolish, did not incontinent persons fear, lest, through the temptation of Satan, they should fall into damnable sins. But whereas he says that he spares them, who he saith will have tribulation of the flesh, there suggests itself to me in the mean while no

sounder interpretation, than that he was unwilling to open, and unfold in words, this selfsame tribulation of the flesh which he fore-announced to those who choose marriage, in suspicions of jealousy of married life, in the begetting and nurture of children, in fears and sorrows of childlessness. For how very few, after they have bound themselves with the bonds of marriage, are not drawn and driven to and fro by these feelings? And this we ought not to exaggerate, lest we spare not the very persons, who the Apostle thought were to be spared.

17. Only by this, which I have briefly set down, the reader ought to be set on his guard against those, who, in this that is written, "but such shall have tribulation of the flesh but I spare you," falsely charge marriage, as indirectly condemned by this sentence; as though he were unwilling to utter the condemnation itself, when he saith, "But I spare you;" so that, forsooth, when he spares them, he spared not his own soul, as saying falsely, "And, if thou shalt have taken a wife, thou hast not sinned; and if a virgin shall have been married, she sinned not." And this, whoso believe or would have believed concerning holy Scripture, they, as it were prepare for themselves a way for liberty of lying, or for defense of their own perverse opinion, in whatever case they hold other sentiments than what sound doctrine demands. For if there shall be alleged any plain statement from the divine books, whereby to refute their errors, this they have at hand as a shield, whereby defending themselves as it were against the truth, they lay themselves bare to be wounded by the devil: to say that the author of the book did not speak the truth in this instance, at one time in order to spare the weak, at another in order to alarm despisers: just as a case

shall come to hand, wherein to defend their own perverse opinion: and thus, whilst they had rather defend than amend their own opinions, they essay to break the authority of holy Scripture, whereby alone all proud and hard necks are broken.

18. Wherefore I admonish both men and women who follow after perpetual continence and holy virginity, that they so set their own good before marriage, as that they judge not marriage an evil: and that they understand that it was in no way of deceit, but of plain truth that it was said by the Apostle, "Whoso gives in marriage does well; and whoso gives not in marriage, does better; and, if thou shalt have taken a wife, thou hast not sinned; and, if a virgin shall have been married, she sinned not;" and a little after, "But she will be more blessed, if she shall have continued so, according to my judgment." And, that the judgment should not be thought human, he adds, "But I think I also have the Spirit of God." This is the doctrine of the Lord, this of the Apostles, this true, this sound, so to choose greater gifts, as that the lesser be not condemned. The truth of God, in the Scripture of God, is better than virginity of man in the mind or flesh of any. Let what is chaste be so loved, as that what is true be not denied. For what evil thought may they not have even concerning their own flesh, who believe that the tongue of the Apostle, in that very place, wherein he was commending virginity of body, was not virgin from corruption of lying. In the first place, therefore, and chiefly, let such as choose the good of virginity, hold most firmly that the holy Scriptures have in nothing spoken lies; and, thus, that that also is true which is said, "And if thou shall have taken a wife, thou hast not sinned; and, if a virgin shall have been

married, she sinned not." And let them not think that the so great good of virgin chastity is made less, if marriage shall not be an evil. Yea rather, let her hence feel confident, rather, that there is prepared for her a palm of greater glory, who feared not to be condemned, in case she were married, but desired to receive a more honorable crown, in that she was not married. Whoso therefore shall be willing to abide without marriage, let them not flee from marriage as a pitfall of sin; but let them surmount it as a hill of the lesser good, in order that they may rest in the mountain of the greater, continence. It is on this condition, forsooth, that this hill is dwelt on; that one leave it not when he will. For, "a woman is bound, so long as her husband lives." However, unto widowed continence one ascends from it as from a step: but for the sake of virgin continence, one must either turn aside from it by not consenting to suitors, or overleap it by anticipating suitors.

19. But lest any should think that of two works, the good and the better, the rewards will be equal, on this account it was necessary to treat against those, who have so interpreted that saying of the Apostle, "But I think that this is good by reason of the present necessity," as to say that virginity is of use not in order to the kingdom of heaven, but in order to this present time: as though in that eternal life, they, who had chosen this better part, would have nothing more than the rest of men. And in this discussion when we came to that saying of the same Apostle, "But such shall have tribulation of the flesh, but I spare you;"2056 we fell in with other disputants, who so far from making marriage equal to perpetual virginity, altogether condemned it. For whereas both are errors,

either to equal marriage to holy virginity, or to condemn it: by fleeing from one another to excess, these two errors come into open collision, in that they have been unwilling to hold the mean of truth: whereby, both by sure reason and authority of holy Scriptures, we both discover that marriage is not a sin, and yet equal it not to the good either of virginal or even of widowed chastity. Some forsooth by aiming at virginity, have thought marriage hateful even as adultery: but others, by defending marriage, would have the excellence of perpetual continence to deserve nothing more than married chastity; as though either the good of Susanna be the lowering of Mary: or the greater good of Mary ought to be the condemnation of Susanna.

20. Far be it, therefore, that the Apostle so said, unto such as are married or are about to marry, "But I spare you," as if he were unwilling to say what punishment is due to the married in another life. Far be it that she, whom Daniel set free from temporal judgment, be cast by Paul into hell! Far be it that her husband's bed be unto her punishment before the judgment seat of Christ, keeping faith to which she chose, under false charge of adultery, to meet either danger, or death! To what effect that speech, "It is better for me to fall into your hands, than to sin in the sight of God:" if God had been about, not to set her free because she kept married chastity, but to condemn her because she had married? And now so often as married chastity is by truth of holy Scripture justified against such as bring calumnies and charges against marriage, so often is Susanna by the Holy Spirit defended against false witnesses, so often is she set free from a false charge, and with much greater ado. For

then against one married woman, now against all; then of hidden and untrue adultery, now of true and open marriage, an accusation is laid. Then one woman, upon what the unjust elders said, now all husbands and wives, upon what the Apostle would not say, are accused. It was, forsooth, your condemnation, say they, that he was silent on, when he said, "But I spare you." Who (saith) this? Surely he, who had said above; "And, if thou shalt have taken a wife, thou hast not sinned; and, if a virgin shall have been married, she sinned not." Why, therefore, wherein he hath been silent through modesty, suspect ye a charge against marriage; and wherein he hath spoken openly, recognize ye not a defense of marriage? What, doth he condemn by his silence them whom he acquitted by his words? Is it not now a milder charge, to charge Susanna, not with marriage, but with adultery itself, than to charge the doctrine of the Apostle with falsehood? What in so great peril could we do, were it not as sure and plain that chaste marriage ought not to be condemned, as it is sure and plain that holy Scripture cannot lie?

21. Here someone will say, What has this to do with holy virginity, or perpetual continence, the setting forth of which was undertaken in this discourse? To whom I make answer in the first place, what I mentioned above, that the glory of that greater good is greater from the fact that, in order to obtain it, the good of married life is surmounted, not the sin of marriage shunned. Otherwise it would be enough for perpetual continence, not to be specially praised, but only not to be blamed: if it were maintained on this account, because it was a crime to wed. In the next place, because it is not by human judgment, but by authority of Divine Scripture, that men

must be exhorted unto so excellent a gift, we must plead not in a common-place manner, or merely by the way, that divine Scripture itself seem not to anyone in any matter to have lied. For they discourage rather than exhort holy virgins, who compel them to continue so by passing sentence on marriage. For whence can they feel sure that that is true, which is written, "And he, who gives her not in marriage, does better:" if they think that false, which yet is written close above, "Both he, who gives his virgin, does well?" But, if they shall without all doubt have believed Scripture speaking of the good of marriage, confirmed by the same most true authority of the divine oracle, they will hasten beyond unto their own better part with glowing and confident eagerness. Wherefore we have already spoken enough for the business which we have taken in hand, and, so far as we could, have shown, that neither that saying of the Apostle, "But I think that this is good by reason of the present necessity," is so to be understood, as though in this life holy virgins are better than faithful women married, but are equal in the kingdom of heaven, and in a future life: nor that other, where he saith of such as wed, "But such shall have tribulation of the flesh, but I spare you;" is to be so understood, as though he chose rather to be silent on, than to speak of, the sin and condemnation of marriage. Forsooth two errors, contrary the one to the other, have, through not understanding them, taken hold of each one of these two sentences. For that concerning the present necessity they interpret in their own favor, who contend to equal such as wed to such as wed not: but this, where it is said, "But I spare you," they who presume to condemn such as wed. But we, according to the faith and sound doctrine of holy Scriptures, both say that marriage is no sin, and yet set its good not only below virginal, but also below widowed continence; and say that the present necessity of married persons is an hindrance to their desert, not indeed unto life eternal, but unto an excellent glory and honor, which is reserved for perpetual continence: and that at this time marriage is not expedient save for such as contain not; and that on the tribulation of the flesh, which cometh from the affection of the flesh, without which marriages of incontinent persons cannot be, the Apostle neither wished to be silent, as forewarning what was true, nor to unfold more fully, as sparing man's weakness.

22. And now by plainest witnesses of divine Scriptures, such as according to the small measure of our memory we shall be able to remember, let it more clearly appear, that, not on account of the present life of this world, but on account of that future life which is promised in the kingdom of heaven, we are to choose perpetual continence. But who but must observe this in that which the same Apostle says a little after, "Whoso is without a wife has thought of the things of the Lord, how to please the Lord: but whoso is joined in marriage has thought of the things of the world, how to please his wife. And a woman unmarried and a virgin is divided; she that is unmarried is careful about the things of the Lord, to be holy both in body and spirit: but she that is married is careful about the things of the world, how to please her husband." Certainly he saith not, hath thought of the things of a state without care in this world, to pass her time without weightier troubles; nor doth he say that a woman unmarried and a virgin is divided, that is, distinguished, and separated from her who is married, for

this end, that the unmarried woman be without care in this life, in order to avoid temporal troubles, which the married woman is not free from: but, "She hath thought," saith he, "of the things of the Lord, how to please the Lord; and is careful about the things of the Lord, to be holy both in body and spirit." Unless to such a degree, perchance, each be foolishly contentious, as to essay to assert, that it is not on account of the kingdom of heaven, but on account of this present world, that we wish to "please the Lord," or that it is on account of this present life, not on account of life eternal, that they are "holy both in body and spirit." To believe this, what else is it, than to be more miserable than all men? For so the Apostle saith, "If in this life only we are hoping in Christ, we are more miserable than all men." What? is he who breaks his bread to the hungry, if he do it only on account of this life, a fool; and shall he be prudent, who chastens his own body even unto continence, whereby he hath no intercourse even in marriage, if it shall profit him naught in the kingdom of heaven?

23. Lastly, let us hear the Lord Himself delivering most plain judgment on this matter. For, upon His speaking after a divine and fearful manner concerning husband and wife not separating, save on account of fornication, His disciples said to Him, "If the case be such with a wife, it is not good to marry." To whom He saith, "Not all receive this saying. For there are eunuchs who were so born: but there are others who were made by men: and there are eunuchs, who made themselves eunuchs for the sake of the kingdom of heaven: whoso can receive, let him receive." What could be said more true, what more clear? Christ saith, the Truth saith, the

Power and Wisdom of God saith, that they, who of pious purpose have contained from marrying a wife, make themselves eunuchs for the sake of the kingdom of heaven: and against this, human vanity with impious rashness contends, that they, who do so, shun only the present necessity of the troubles of married life, but in the kingdom of heaven have no more than others.

24. But concerning what eunuchs speak God by the prophet Isaiah, unto whom He saith that He will give in His house and in His wall a place by name, much better than of sons and daughters, save concerning these, who make themselves eunuchs for the sake of the kingdom of heaven? For these, whose bodily organ is without strength, so that they cannot beget, (such as are the eunuchs of rich men and of kings,) it is surely enough, when they become Christians, and keep the commands of God, yet have this purpose, that, if they could, they would have wives, to be made equal to the rest of the faithful in the house of God, who are married, who bring up in the fear of God a family which they have lawfully and chastely gotten, teaching their sons to set their hope on God; but not to receive a better place than of sons and daughters. For it is not of virtue of the soul, but of necessity of the flesh, that they marry not wives. Let who will contend that the Prophet foretold this of those eunuchs who have suffered mutilation of body; that even also helps the cause which we have undertaken. For God hath not preferred these eunuchs to such as have no place in His house, but assuredly to those who keep the desert of married life in begetting sons. For, when He saith, "I will give unto them a place much better;" He shows that one is also given unto the married, but much inferior.

Therefore, to allow that in the house of God there will be the eunuchs after the flesh spoken of above, who were not in the People of Israel: because we see that these also themselves, whereas they become not Jews, yet become Christians: and that the Prophet spoke not of them, who through purpose of continence seeking not marriage, make themselves eunuchs for the sake of the kingdom of heaven: is anyone so madly opposed to the truth as to believe that eunuchs made so in the flesh have a better place than married persons in the house of God, and to contend that persons being of pious purpose continent, chastening the body even unto contempt of marriage, making themselves eunuchs, not in the body, but in the very root of concupiscence, practicing an heavenly and angelic life in an earthly mortal state, are on a level with the deserts of the married; and, being a Christian, to gainsay Christ when He praises those who have made themselves eunuchs, not for the sake of this world, but for the sake of the kingdom of heaven, affirming that this is of use for the present life, not for a future? What else remains for these, save to assert that the kingdom of heaven itself pertains unto this temporal life, wherein we now are? For why should not blind presumption advance even to this madness? And what fuller of frenzy than this assertion? For, although at times the Church, even that which is at this time, is called the kingdom of heaven; certainly it is so called for this end, because it is being gathered together for a future and eternal life. Although, therefore, it have the promise of the present, and of a future life, yet in all its good works it looks not to "the things that are seen, but to what are not seen. For what are seen are temporal; but what are not seen, are eternal."

25. Nor indeed hath the Holy Spirit failed to speak what should be of open and unshaken avail against these men, most shamelessly and madly obstinate, and should repel their assault, as of wild beasts, from His sheep-fold, by defenses that may not be stormed. For, after He had said concerning eunuchs, "I will give unto them in My house and in My wall a named place, much better than of sons and daughters;" lest any too carnal should think that there was anything temporal to be hoped for in these words, straightway He added, "An eternal name I will give unto them, nor shall it ever fail:" as though He should say, Why dost thou draw back, impious blindness? Why dost thou draw back? Why dost thou pour the clouds of thy perverseness over the clear (sky) of truth? Why in so great light of Scriptures dost thou seek after darkness from out which to lay snares? Why dost thou promise temporal advantage only to holy persons exercising continence? "An eternal name I will give unto them:" why, where persons keep from all sexual intercourse, and also in the very fact that they abstain from these, have thought of the things of the Lord, how to please the Lord, do you essay to refer them unto earthly advantage? "An eternal name I will give unto them." Why contend you that the kingdom of heaven, for the sake of which holy eunuchs have made themselves eunuchs, is to be understood in this life only? "An eternal name I will give unto them." And if haply in this place you endeavor to take the word itself eternal in the sense of lasting for a long time, I add, I heap up, I tread in, "nor shall it ever fail." What more seek you? What more say you? This eternal name, whatever it be, unto the eunuchs of God, which assuredly signifies a certain peculiar and excellent glory, shall not be in common with many, although set in

the same kingdom, and in the same house. For on this account also, perhaps, it is called a name, that it distinguishes those, to whom it is given, from the rest.

26. What then, say they, is the meaning of that penny, which is given in payment to all alike when the work of the vineyard is ended? whether it be to those who have labored from the first hour, or to those who have labored one hour? What assuredly doth it signify, but something, which all shall have in common, such as is life eternal itself, the kingdom of heaven itself, where shall be all, whom God hath predestinated, called, justified, glorified? "For it behooved that this corruptible put on incorruption, and this mortal put on immortality." This is that penny, wages for all. Yet "star differed from star in glory; so also the resurrection of the dead." These are the different merits of the Saints. For, if by that penny the heaven were signified, have not all the stars in common to be in the heaven? And yet, "There is one glory of the sun, another glory of the moon, another of the stars." If that penny were taken for health of body, have not all the members, when we are well, health in common; and, should this health continue even unto death, is it not in all alike and equally? And yet, "God hath set the members, each one of them, in the body, as He would;" that neither the whole be an eye, nor the whole hearing, nor the whole smelling: and, whatever else there is, it hath its own property, although it have health equally with all. Thus because life eternal itself shall be alike to all, an equal penny was assigned to all; but, because in that life eternal itself the lights of merits shall shine with a distinction, there are "many mansions" in the house of the Father: and, by this means, in the penny not unlike, one lives not

longer than another; but in the many mansions, one is honored with greater brightness than another.

27. Therefore go on, Saints of God, boys and girls, males and females, unmarried men, and women; go on and persevere unto the end. Praise more sweetly the Lord, Whom ye think on more richly: hope more happily in Him, Whom ye serve more instantly: love more ardently Him, whom ye please more attentively. With loins girded, and lamps burning, wait for the Lord, when He cometh from the marriage. Ye shall bring unto the marriage of the Lamb a new song, which ye shall sing on your harps. Not surely such as the whole earth sings, unto which it is said, "Sing unto the Lord a new song; sing unto the Lord, the whole earth": but such as no one shall be able to utter but you. For thus there saw you in the Apocalypse a certain one beloved above others by the Lamb, who had been wanting to lie on His breast, and who used to drink in, and burst forth, the Word of God above wonders of heaven. He saw you twelve times twelve thousand of holy harpers, of undefiled virginity in body, of inviolate truth in heart; and he wrote of you, that ye follow the Lamb whithersoever He shall go. Where think we that This Lamb goes, where no one either dares or is able to follow save you? Where think we that He goes? Into what glades and meadows? Where, I think, the grass are joys; not vain joys of this world, lying madnesses; nor joys such as shall be in the kingdom of God itself, for the rest that are not virgins; but distinct from the portion of joys of all the rest. Joy of the virgins of Christ, of Christ, in Christ, with Christ, after Christ, through Christ, for Christ. The joys peculiar to the virgins of Christ, are not the same as of such as are not virgins, although of Christ. For there are to

different persons different joys, but to none such. Go (enter) into these, follow the Lamb, because the Flesh of the Lamb also is assuredly virgin. For this He retained in Himself when grown up, which He took not away from His Mother by His conception and birth. Follow Him, as ye deserve, in virginity of heart and flesh, wheresoever He shall have gone. For what is it to follow, but to imitate? Because "Christ hath suffered for us," leaving us an example, as saith the Apostle Peter, "that we should follow His steps." Him each one follows in that, wherein he imitates Him: not so far forth as He is the only Son of God, by Whom all things were made; but so far forth as, the Son of Man, He set forth in Himself, what behooved for us to imitate. And many things in Him are set forth for all to imitate: but virginity of the flesh not for all; for they have not what to do in order to be virgins, in whom it hath been already brought to pass that they be not virgins.

28. Therefore let the rest of the faithful, who have lost virginity, follow the Lamb, not whithersoever He shall have gone, but so far as ever they shall have been able. But they are able everywhere, save when He walks in the grace of virginity. "Blessed are the poor in spirit;" imitate Him, Who, whereas "He was rich, was made poor for your sakes." "Blessed are the meek;" imitate Him, Who said, "Learn of Me, for I am meek and lowly of heart." "Blessed are they that mourn;" imitate Him, Who "wept over" Jerusalem. "Blessed are they, who hunger and thirst after righteousness;" imitate Him, Who said, "My meat is to do the will of Him Who sent Me." "Blessed are the merciful;" imitate Him, Who came to the help of him who was wounded by robbers, and who lay in the way halfdead and despaired of. "Blessed are the pure

in heart;" imitate Him, "Who did no sin, neither was guile found in His mouth." "Blessed are the peace-makers;" imitate Him, Who said on behalf of His persecutors, "Father, forgive them, for they know not what they do." "Blessed are they, who suffer persecution for righteousness sake;" imitate Him, Who "suffered for you, leaving you an example, that ye follow His steps." These things, whoso imitate, in these they follow the Lamb. But surely even married persons may go in those steps, although not setting their foot perfectly in the same print, yet walking in the same paths.

    29. But, lo, That Lamb goes by a Virgin road, how shall they go after Him, who have lost what there is no way for them to recover? Do ye, therefore, do ye go after Him, His virgins; do ye thither also go after Him, in that on this one account whithersoever He shall have gone, ye follow Him: for unto any other gift whatsoever of holiness, whereby to follow Him, we can exhort married persons, save this which they have lost beyond power of recovery. Do ye, therefore, follow Him, by holding with perseverance what ye have vowed with ardor. Go when ye can, that the good of virginity perish not from you, unto which ye can do nothing, in order that it may return. The rest of the multitude of the faithful will see you, which cannot unto this follow the Lamb; it will see you, it will not envy you: and by rejoicing together with you, what it hath not in itself, it will have in you. For that new song also, which is your own, it will not be able to utter; but it will not be unable to hear, and to be delighted with your so excellent good: but ye, who shall both utter and hear, in that what ye shall say, this ye shall hear of yourselves, will exult with greater happiness, and reign with greater

joy. But they will have no sorrow on account of your greater joy, to whom this shall be wanting. Forsooth That Lamb, Whom ye shall follow whithersoever He shall have gone, will not desert those who cannot follow Him, where you can. Almighty is the Lamb, of Whom we speak. He both will go before you, and will not depart from them, when God shall be all in all. And they, who shall have less, shall not turn away in dislike from you: for, where there is no envying, difference exists with concord. Take to you, then, have trust, be strong, continue, ye who vow and pay unto the Lord your God vows of perpetual continence, not for the sake of this present world, but for the sake of the kingdom of Heaven.

30. Ye also who have not yet made this vow, who are able to receive it, receive it. Run with perseverance, that ye may obtain. Take ye each his sacrifices, and enter ye into the courts of the Lord, not of necessity, having power over your own will. For not as, "Thou shall not commit adultery, Thou shall not kill," can it so be said, Thou shalt not wed. The former are demanded, the latter are offered. If the latter are done, they are praised: unless the former are done, they are condemned. In the former the Lord commands us what is due; but in the latter, if ye shall have spent anything more, on His return He will repay you. Think of (whatever that be) within His wall "a place named, much better than of sons and of daughters." Think of "an eternal name" there. Who unfolds of what kind that name shall be? Yet, whatever it shall be, it shall be eternal. By believing and hoping and loving this, ye have been able, not to shun marriage, as forbidden, but to fly past it, as allowed.

31. Whence the greatness of this service, unto the undertaking of which we have according to our strength exhorted, the more excellent and divine it is, the more doth it warn our anxiety, to say something not only concerning most glorious chastity, but also concerning safest humility. When then such as make profession of perpetual chastity, comparing themselves with married persons, shall have discovered, that, according to the Scriptures, the others are below both in work and wages, both in vow and reward, let what is written straightway come into their mind, "By how much thou art great, by so much humble thyself in all things: and thou shalt find favor before God. "The measure of humility for each hath been given from the measure of his greatness itself: unto which pride is full of danger, which laid the greater wait against persons the greater they be. On this followed envying, as a daughter in her train; forsooth pride straightway giveth birth to her, nor is she ever without such a daughter and companion. By which two evils, that is, pride and envying, is the devil (a devil). Therefore, it is against pride, the mother of envying, that the whole Christian discipline chiefly wars. For this teaches humility, whereby both to gain and to keep charity; of which after that it had been said, "Charity envied not;" as though we were asking the reason, how it comes to pass that it envied not, he straightway added, "is not puffed up;" as though he should say, on this account it hath not envying, in that neither hath it pride. Therefore the Teacher of humility, Christ, first "emptied Himself, taking the form of a servant, made in the likeness of men, and found in fashion as a man, He humbled Himself, made obedient even unto death, even the death of the Cross." But His teaching itself, how carefully it suggests humility,

and how earnest and instant it is in commanding this, who can easily unfold, and bring together all witnesses for proof of this matter? This let him essay to do, or do, whosoever shall wish to write a separate treatise on humility; but of this present work the end proposed is different, and it hath been undertaken on a matter so great, as that it hath chiefly to guard against pride.

32. Wherefore a few witnesses, which the Lord deigns to suggest to my mind, I proceed to mention, from out the teaching of Christ concerning humility, such as perhaps may be enough for my purpose. His discourse, the first which He delivered to His disciples at greater length, began from this. "Blessed are the poor in spirit, for theirs is the Kingdom of Heaven." And these without all controversy we take to be humble. The faith of that Centurion He on this account chiefly praised, and said that He had not found in Israel so great faith, because he believed with so great humility as to say, "I am not worthy that thou shouldest enter under my roof." Whence also Matthew for no other reason said that he "came" unto Jesus, (whereas Luke most plainly signifies that he came not unto Him himself, but sent his friends,) save that by his most faithful humility he himself came unto Him more than they whom he sent. Whence also is that of the Prophet, "The Lord is very high, and hath respect unto things that are lowly: but what are very high He noted afar off;" assuredly as not coming unto Him. Whence also He saith to that woman of Canaan, "O woman, great is thy faith; be it done unto thee as thou wilt;" whom above He had called a dog, and had made answer that the bread of the sons was not to be cast to her. And this she taking with humility had said, "Even so, Lord; for the dogs also

eat of the crumbs which fall from their masters' table." And thus what by continual crying she obtained not, by humble confession she earned. Hence also those two are set forth praying in the Temple, the one a Pharisee, and the other a Publican, for the sake of those who seem to themselves just and despise the rest of men, and the confession of sins is set before the reckoning up of merits. And assuredly the Pharisee was rendering thanks unto God by reason of those things wherein he was greatly self-satisfied. "I render thanks to Thee," saith he, "that I am not even as the rest of men, unjust, extortioners, adulterers, even as also this publican. I fast twice in the week, I give tithes of all things whatsoever I possess. But the Publican was standing afar off, not daring to lift up his eyes to Heaven, but beating his breast, saying, God be merciful unto me a sinner." But there follows the divine judgment, "Verily I say unto you, the Publican went down from the Temple justified more than that Pharisee." Then the cause is shown, why this is just; "Forasmuch as he who exalted himself shall be humbled, and whoso humbled himself shall be exalted." Therefore it may come to pass, that each one both shun real evils, and reflect on real goods in himself, and render thanks for these unto "the Father of lights, from Whom cometh down every best gift, and every perfect gift," and yet be rejected by reason of the sin of haughtiness, if through pride, even in his thought alone, which is before God, he insult other sinners, and especially when confessing their sins in prayer, unto whom is due not upbraiding with arrogance, but pity without despair. What is it that, when His disciples were questioning among themselves, who of them should be greater, He set a little child before their eyes, saying, "Unless ye shall be as this child, ye shall not enter into the Kingdom of Heaven?" Did He not chiefly commend humility, and set in it the desert of greatness? Or when unto the sons of Zebedee desiring to be at His side in lofty seats He so made answer, as that they should rather think of having to drink the Cup of His Passion, wherein He humbled Himself even unto death, even the death of the Cross, than with proud desire demand to be preferred to the rest; what did He show, save, that He would be a bestower of exaltation upon them, who should first follow Him as a teacher of humility? And now, in that, when about to go forth unto His Passion, He washed the feet of His disciples, and most openly taught them to do for their fellow-disciples and fellow-servants this, which He their Lord and Master had done for them; how greatly did He commend humility? And in order to commend this He chose also that time, wherein they were looking on Him, as immediately about to die, with great longing; assuredly about to retain in their memory this especially, which their Master, Whom they were to imitate, had pointed out to them as the last thing. But He did this at that time, which surely He could have done on other days also before, wherein He had been conversant with them; at which time if it were done, this same would indeed be delivered, but certainly would not be so received.

33. Whereas, then, all Christians have to guard humility, forasmuch as it is from Christ that they are called Christians, Whose Gospel no one considers with care, but that he discovers Him to be a Teacher of humility; specially is it becoming that they be followers and keepers of this virtue, who excel the rest of men in any great good, in order that they may have a great care of

that, which I set down in the beginning, "By how much thou art great, by so much humble thyself in all things, and thou shall find grace before God." Wherefore, because perpetual Continence and specially virginity, is a great good in the Saints of God, they must with all watchfulness beware, that it be not corrupted with pride.

34. Paul the Apostle censures evil unmarried women, curious and prating, and says that this fault comes of idleness. "But at the same time," saith he, "being idle they learn to go about to houses: but not only idle, but curious also and prating, speaking what they ought not." Of these he had said above, "But younger widows avoid; for when they have past their time in delights, they wish to wed in Christ; having condemnation, in that they have made void their first faith:" that is, have not continued in that, which they had vowed at the first. And yet he saith not, they marry, but "they wish to marry." For many of them are recalled from marrying, not by love of a noble purpose, but by fear of open shame, which also itself comes of pride, whereby persons fear to displease men more than God. These, therefore, who wish to marry, and do not marry on this account, because they cannot with impunity, who would do better to marry than to be burned, that is, than to be laid waste in their very conscience by the hidden flame of lust, who repent of their profession, and who feel their confession irksome; unless they correct and set right their heart, and by the fear of God again overcome their lust, must be accounted among the dead; whether they pass their time in delights, whence the Apostle says, "But she who passes her time in delights, living, is dead;" or whether in labors and fastings, which are useless where

there is no correction of the heart, and serve rather for display than amendment. I do not, for my part, impose on such a great regard for humility, in whom pride itself is confounded, and bloodstained by wound of conscience. Nor on such as are drunken, or covetous, or who are lying in any other kind whatever of damnable disease, at the same time that they have profession of bodily continence, and through perverse manners are at variance with their own name, do I impose this great anxiety about pious humility: unless haply in these evils they shall dare even to make a display of themselves, unto whom it is not enough, that the punishments of these are deferred. Nor am I treating of these, in whom there is a certain aim of pleasing, either by more elegant dress than the necessity of so great profession demands, or by remarkable manner of binding the head, whether by bosses of hair swelling forth, or by coverings so yielding, that the fine network below appears: unto these we must give precepts, not as yet concerning humility, but concerning chastity itself, or virgin modesty. Give me one who makes profession of perpetual continence, and who is free from these, and all such faults and spots of conduct; for this one I fear pride, for this so great good I am in alarm from the swelling of arrogance. The more there is in any one on account of which to be self-pleased, the more I fear, lest, by pleasing self, he please not Him, Who "resisted the proud, but unto the humble giveth grace."

35. Certainly we are to contemplate in Christ Himself, the chief instruction and pattern of virginal purity. What further precept then concerning humility shall I give to the continent, than what He saith to all, "Learn of Me, in that I am meek and lowly of heart?"

when He had made mention above of His greatness, and, wishing to show this very thing, how great He was, and how little He had been made for our sakes, saith, "I confess to Thee, O Father, Lord of heaven and earth, in that Thou hast hidden these things from the wise and prudent, and hast revealed them unto little children. Even so, O Father, in that so it hath been pleasing before Thee. All things have been delivered unto Me of My Father: and no one knows the Son, save the Father; and no one knows the Father, save the Son, and he to whom the Son shall have willed to reveal Him. Come unto Me, all ye who labor and are burdened, and I will refresh you. Take My yoke upon you, and learn of Me, in that I am meek and lowly of heart." He, He, unto Whom the Father hath delivered all things, and Whom no one knows but the Father, and Who alone, (and he, unto whom He shall have willed to reveal Him), knows the Father, saith not, "Learn of Me" to make the world, or to raise the dead, but, "in that I am meek and lowly of heart." O saving teaching? O Teacher and Lord of mortals, unto whom death was pledged and passed on in the cup of pride, He would not teach what Himself was not, He would not bid what Himself did not. I see Thee, O good Jesu, with the eyes of faith, which Thou hast opened for me, as in an assembly of the human race, crying out and saying, "Come unto Me, and learn of Me." What, I beseech Thee, through Whom all things were made, O Son of God, and the Same Who was made among all things, O Son of Man: to learn what of Thee, come we to Thee? "For that I am meek," saith He, "and lowly of heart." Is it to this that all the treasures of wisdom and knowledge hidden in Thee are brought, that we learn this of Thee as a great thing, that Thou art "meek and lowly of heart?" Is it so great a thing to be little, that it could not at all be learned unless it were brought to pass by Thee, Who art so great? So indeed it is. For by no other way is there found out rest for the soul, save when the unquiet swelling hath been dispersed, whereby it was great unto itself, when it was not sound unto Thee.

36. Let them hear Thee, and let them come to Thee, and let them learn of Thee to be meek and lowly, who seek Thy Mercy and Truth, by living unto Thee, unto Thee, not unto themselves. Let him hear this, laboring and laden, who is weighed down by his burthen, so as not to dare to lift up his eyes to heaven, that sinner beating his breast, and drawing near from afar. Let him hear, the centurion, not worthy that Thou shouldest enter under his roof. Let him hear, Zaccheus, chief of publicans, restoring fourfold the gains of damnable sins. Let her hear, the woman in the city a sinner, by so much the more full of tears at Thy feet, the more alien she had been from Thy steps. Let them hear, the harlots and publicans, who enter into the kingdom of heaven before the Scribes and Pharisees. Let them hear, every kind of such ones, feastings with whom were cast in Thy teeth as a charge, forsooth, as though by whole persons who sought not a physician, whereas Thou comes not to call the righteous, but sinners to repentance. All these, when they are converted unto Thee, easily grow meek, and are humbled before Thee, mindful of their own most unrighteous life, and of Thy most indulgent mercy, in that, "where sin hath abounded, grace hath abounded more."

37. But regard the troops of virgins, holy boys and girls: this kind hath been trained up in Thy Church: there

for Thee it hath been budding from its mother's breasts; for Thy Name it hath loosed its tongue to speak, Thy Name, as through the milk of its infancy, it hath had poured in and hath sucked, no one of this number can say, "I, who before was a blasphemer, and persecutor, and injurious, but I obtained mercy, in that I did in being ignorant, in unbelief." Yea more, that, which Thou commanded not, but only didst set forth, for such as would, to seize, saying, "Whoso can receive, let him receive;" they have seized, they have vowed, and, for the sake of the kingdom of heaven, not for that Thou threatened, but for that Thou exhorted, they have made themselves eunuchs. To these cry out, let these hear Thee, in that Thou art "meek and lowly of heart." Let these, by how much they are great, by so much humble themselves in all things, that they may find grace before Thee. They are just: but they are not, are they, such as Thou, justifying the ungodly? They are chaste: but them in sins their mothers nurtured in their wombs. They are holy, but Thou art also Holy of Holies. They are virgins, but they are not also born of virgins. They are wholly chaste both in spirit and in flesh: but they are not the Word made flesh. And yet let them learn, not from those unto whom Thou forgives sins, but from Thee Thyself, The Lamb of God Who takes away the sins of the world, in that Thou art "meek and lowly of heart."

38. I send thee not, soul that art religiously chaste, that hast not given the reins to fleshly appetite even so far as to allowed marriage, that hast not indulged thy body about to depart even to the begetting one to succeed thee, that hast sustained aloft thy earthly members, afloat to accustom them to heaven; I send thee not, in order that

thou mayest learn humility, unto publicans and sinners, who yet enter into the kingdom of heaven before the proud: I send thee not to these: for they, who have been set free from the gulf of uncleanness, are unworthy that undefiled virginity be sent to them to take pattern from. I send thee unto the King of Heaven, unto Him, by Whom men were created, and Who was created among men for the sake of men; unto Him, Who is fair of beauty above the sons of men, and despised by the sons of men on behalf of the sons of men: unto Him, Who, ruling the immortal angels, disdained not to do service unto mortals. Him, at any rate, not unrighteousness, but charity, made humble; "Charity, which rivaled not, is not puffed up, seeks not her own;" forasmuch as "Christ also pleased not Himself, but, as it is written of Him, The reproaches of such as reproached Thee have fallen upon Me." Go then, come unto Him, and learn, in that He is "meek and lowly of heart." Thou shall not go unto him, who dared not by reason of the burden of unrighteousness to lift up his eyes to heaven, but unto Him, Who by the weight of charity came down from heaven. Thou shalt not go unto her, who watered with tears the feet of her Lord, seeking forgiveness of heavy sins; but thou shalt go unto Him, Who, granting forgiveness of all sins, washed the feet of His own disciples. I know the dignity of thy virginity; I propose not to thee to imitate the Publican humbly accusing his own faults; but I fear for the Pharisee proudly boasting of his own merits. I say not, Be thou such as she, of whom it was said, "There are forgiven unto her many sins, in that she hath loved much;" but I fear lest, as thinking that thou hast little forgiven to thee, thou love little.

39. I fear, I say, greatly for thee, lest, when thou boasts that thou wilt follow the Lamb wheresoever He shall have gone, thou be unable by reason of swelling pride to follow Him through strait ways. It is good for thee, O virgin soul, that thus, as thou art a virgin, thus altogether keeping in thy heart that thou hast been born again, keeping in thy flesh that thou hast been born, thou yet conceive of the fear of the Lord, and give birth to the spirit of salvation. "Fear," indeed, "there is not in charity, but perfect charity," as it is written, "casted out fear:" but fear of men, not of God: fear of temporal evils, not of the Divine Judgment at the last. "Be not thou high-minded, but fear." Love thou the goodness of God; fear thou His severity: neither suffers thee to be proud. For by loving you fear, lest you grievously offend One Who is loved and loves. For what more grievous offense, than that by pride thou displease Him, Who for thy sake hath been displeasing to the proud? And where ought there to be more that "chaste fear abiding for ever and ever," than in thee, who hast no thought of the things of this world, how to please a wedded partner; but of the things of the Lord, how to please the Lord? That other fear is not in charity, but this chaste fear quitted not charity. If you love not, fear lest you perish; if you love, fear lest you displease. That fear charity casted out, with this it runs within. The Apostle Paul also says, "For we have not received the spirit of bondage again to fear; but we have received the spirit of adoption of sons, wherein we cry, Abba, Father." I believe that he speaks of that fear, which had been given in the Old Testament, lest the temporal goods should be lost, which God had promised unto those not yet sons under grace, but as yet slaves under the law. There is also the fear of eternal fire, to serve God in order to avoid

which is assuredly not yet of perfect charity. For the desire of the reward is one thing, the fear of punishment another. They are different sayings, "Whither shall I go away from Thy Spirit, and from Thy face whither shall I flee?" and, "One thing I have sought of the Lord, this I will seek after; that I may dwell in the house of the Lord through all the days of my life, that I may consider the delight of the Lord, that I be protected in His temple:" and, "Turn not away Thy face from me:" and, "My soul longs and faints unto the courts of the Lord." Those sayings let him have had, who dared not to lift up his eyes to heaven; and she who was watering with tears His feet, in order to obtain pardon for her grievous sins; but these do thou have, who art careful about the things of the Lord, to be holy both in body and spirit. With those sayings there companies fear which hath torment, which perfect charity casted forth; but with these sayings there companies chaste fear of the Lord, that abides forever and ever. And to both kinds it must be said, "Be not thou high-minded, but fear;" that man neither of defense of his sins, nor of presumption of righteousness set himself up. For Paul also himself, who saith, "For ye have not received the spirit of bondage again to fear;" yet, fear being a companion of charity, saith, "With fear and much trembling was I towards you:" and that saying, which I have mentioned, that the engrafted wild olive tree be not proud against the broken branches of the olive tree, himself made use of, saying, "Be not thou high-minded, but fear;" himself admonishing all the members of Christ in general, saith, "With fear and trembling work out your own salvation; for it is God Who worketh in you both to will and to do, according to His good pleasure;" that it seem not to pertain unto the Old Testament what is

Of Holy Virginity

written, "Serve the Lord in fear, and rejoice unto Him with trembling."

40. And what members of the holy body, which is the Church, ought more to take care, that upon them the holy Spirit may rest, than such as profess virginal holiness? But how doth He rest, where He finds not His own place? what else than an humbled heart, to fill, not to leap back from; to raise up, not to weigh down? whereas it hath been most plainly said, "On whom shall rest My Spirit? On him that is humble and quiet, and trembles at My words." Already thou lives righteously, already thou lives piously, thou lives chastely, holily, with virginal purity; as yet, however, thou lives here, and art thou not humbled at hearing, "What, is not human life upon earth a trial?" Does it not drive thee back from over-confident arrogance, "Woe unto the world because of offenses?" Does thou not tremble, lest thou be accounted among the many, whose "love waxed cold, because that iniquity abounds?" Does thou not smite thy breast, when thou hears, "Wherefore, whoso thinketh that he stands, let him see to it lest he fall?" Amid these divine warnings and human dangers, do we yet find it so hard to persuade holy virgins to humility?

41. Or are we indeed to believe that it is for any other reason, that God suffers to be mixed up with the number of your profession, many, both men and women, about to fall, than that by the fall of these your fear may be increased, whereby to repress pride; which God so hates, as that against this one thing The Highest humbled Himself? Unless haply, in truth, thou shalt therefore fear less, and be more puffed up, so as to love little Him, Who

hath loved thee so much, as to give up Himself for thee, because He hath forgiven thee little, living, forsooth from childhood, religiously, piously, with pious chastity, with inviolate virginity. As though in truth you ought not to love with much greater glow of affection Him, Who, whatsoever things He hath forgiven unto sinners upon their being turned to Him, suffered you not to fall into them. Or indeed that Pharisee, who therefore loved little, because he thought that little was forgiven him, was it for any other reason that he was blinded by this error, than because being ignorant of the righteousness of God, and seeking to establish his own, he had not been made subject unto the righteousness of God? But you, an elect race, and among the elect more elect, virgin choirs that follow the Lamb, even you "by grace have been saved through faith; and this not of yourselves, but it is the gift of God: not of works, lest haply any be elated. For we are His workmanship, created in Jesus Christ in good works, which God hath prepared, that in them we may walk." What therefore, by how much the more ye are adorned by His gifts, shall ye by so much the less love Him? May He Himself turn away so dreadful madness! Wherefore forasmuch as the Truth has spoken the truth, that he, unto whom little is forgiven, loveth little; do ye, in order that ye may love with full glow of affection Him, Whom ye are free to love, being loosened from ties of marriage, account as altogether forgiven unto you, whatever of evil, by His governance, ye have not committed. For "your eyes ever unto the Lord, forasmuch as He shall pluck out of the net your feet," and, "Except the Lord shall have kept the city, in vain hath he watched who kept it." And speaking of Continence itself the Apostle says, "But I would that all men were as I myself; but each one hath his own proper gift from God; one in this way, and another in that way." Who therefore bestowed these gifts? Who distributed his own proper gifts unto each as He will? Forsooth God, with Whom there is not unrighteousness, and by this means with what equity He makes some in this way, and others in that way, for man to know is either impossible or altogether hard: but that with equity He makes, it is not lawful to doubt. "What," therefore, "hast thou, which thou hast not received?" And by what perversity dost thou less love Him, of Whom thou hast received more?

42. Wherefore let this be the first thought for the putting on of humility, that God's virgin think not that it is of herself that she is such, and not rather that this best "gift cometh down from above from the Father of Lights, with Whom is no change nor shadow of motion." For thus she will not think that little hath been forgiven her, so as for her to love little, and, being ignorant of the righteousness of God, and wishing to establish her own, not to be made subject to the righteousness of God. In which fault was that Simon who was surpassed by the woman, unto whom many sins were forgiven, because she loved much. But she will have more cautious and true thoughts, that we are so to account all sins as though forgiven, from which God keeps us that we commit them not. Witnesses are those expressions of pious prayers in holy Scriptures, whereby it is shown, that those very things, which are commanded by God, are not done save by His Gift and help, Who commands. For there is a falsehood in the asking for them, if we could do them without the help of His grace. What is there so generally and chiefly charged, as obedience whereby the

Commandments of God are kept? And yet we find this wished for. "Thou," saith he, "hast charged, that Thy commandments be greatly kept." Then it follows, "O that my ways were directed to keep Thy righteousnesses: then shall I not be confounded, whilst I look unto all Thy commandments." That which he had set down above that God had commanded, that he wished might of himself be fulfilled. This is done assuredly, that there be not sin; but, if there hath been sin, the command is that one repent; lest by defense and excuse of sin he perish through pride, who hath done it, whilst he is unwilling that what he hath done perish through repentance. This also is asked of God, so that it may be understood that it is not done, save by His grant from Whom it is asked. "Set," saith he, "O Lord, a watch to my mouth, and a door of continence around my lips: let not my heart turn away unto evil words, to make excuses in sins, with men that work unrighteousness." If, therefore, both obedience, whereby we keep His commandments, and repentance whereby we excuse not our sins, are wished for and asked, it is plain that, when it is done, it is by His gift that it is possessed, by His help that it is fulfilled, yet more openly is it said by reason of obedience, "By the Lord the steps of a man are directed, and He shall will His way:" and of repentance the Apostle says, "if haply God may grant unto them repentance."

43. Concerning continence also itself hath it not been most openly said, "And when I knew that no one can be continent unless God give it, this also itself was a part of wisdom, to know whose gift it was?" But perhaps continence is the gift of God, but wisdom man bestows upon himself, whereby to understand, that that gift is, not his own, but of God. Yea, "The Lord makes wise the

blind:" and, "The testimony of the Lord is faithful, it giveth wisdom unto little ones:" and, "If anyone want wisdom, let him ask of God, Who giveth unto all liberally, and upbraided not, and it shall be given to him." But it becometh virgins to be wise, that their lamps be not extinguished. How "wise," save "not having high thoughts, but consenting unto the lowly." For Wisdom Itself hath said unto man, "Lo, piety is wisdom!" If therefore thou hast nothing, which thou hast not received, "Be not high-minded, but fear." And love not thou little, as though Him by Whom little hath been forgiven to thee; but, rather, love Him much, by Whom much hath been given to thee. For if he loves, unto whom it hath been given not to repay: how much more ought he to love, unto whom it hath been given to possess. For both, whosoever continues chaste from the beginning, is ruled by Him; and whosoever is made chaste instead of unchaste, is corrected by Him; and whosoever is unchaste even unto the end, is abandoned by Him. But this He can do by secret counsel, by unrighteous He cannot: and perhaps it is for this end that it lies hid, that there may be more fear, and less pride.

44. Next let not man, now that he knows that by the grace of God he is what he is, fall into another snare of pride, so as by lifting up himself for the very grace of God to despise the rest. By which fault that other Pharisee both gave thanks unto God for the goods which he had, and yet vaunted himself above the Publican confessing his sins. What therefore should a virgin do, what should she think, that she vaunt not herself above those, men or women, who have not this so great gift? For she ought not to feign humility, but to set it forth: for the feigning of

humility is greater pride. Wherefore Scripture wishing to show that humility ought to be true, after having said, "By how much thou art great, by so much humble thyself in all things," added soon after, "And thou shalt find grace before God:" assuredly where one could not humble one's self deceitfully.

45. Wherefore what shall we say? is there any thought which a virgin of God may truly have, by reason of which she dare not to set herself before a faithful woman, not only a widow, but even married? I say not a reprobate virgin; for who knows not that an obedient woman is to be set before a disobedient virgin? But where both are obedient unto the commands of God, shall she so tremble to prefer holy virginity even to chaste marriage, and continence to wedded life, the fruit a hundred-fold to go before the thirty-fold? Nay, let her not doubt to prefer this thing to that thing; yet let not this or that virgin, obeying and fearing God, dare to set herself before this or that woman, obeying and fearing God; otherwise she will not be humble, and "God resisted the proud!" What, therefore, shall she have in her thoughts? Forsooth the hidden gifts of God, which naught save the questioning of trial makes known to each, even in himself. For, to pass over the rest, whence doth a virgin know, although careful of the things of the Lord, how to please the Lord but that haply, by reason of some weakness of mind unknown to herself, she be not as yet ripe for martyrdom, whereas that woman, whom she rejoiced to set herself before, may already be able to drink the Cup of the Lord's humiliation, which He set before His disciples, to drink first, when enamored of high place? Whence, I say, doth she know but that she herself be not as yet Thecla, that

other be already Crispina. Certainly unless there be present trial, there takes place no proof of this gift.

46. But this is so great, that certain understand it to be the fruit a hundred-fold. For the authority of the Church bears a very conspicuous witness, in which it is known to the faithful in what place the Martyrs, in what place the holy nuns deceased, are rehearsed at the Sacraments of the Altar. But what the meaning is of that difference of fruitfulness, let them see to it, who understand these things better than we; whether the virginal life be in fruit an hundred-fold, in sixty-fold the widowed, in thirty-fold the married; or whether the hundred-fold fruitfulness be ascribed unto martyrdom, the sixty-fold unto continence, the thirty-fold unto marriage; or whether virginity, by the addition of martyrdom, fill up the hundred-fold, but when alone be in sixty-fold, but married persons bearing thirty-fold arrive at sixty-fold, in case they shall be martyrs: or whether, what seems to me more probable, forasmuch as the gifts of Divine grace are many, and one is greater and better than another, whence the Apostle says, "But emulate ye the better gifts;" we are to understand that they are more in number than to allow of being distributed under those different kinds. In the first place, that we set not widowed continence either as bearing no fruit, or set it but level with the desert of married charity, or equal it unto virgin glory; or think that the Crown of Martyrdom, either established in habit of mind, although proof of trial be wanting, or in actual making trial of suffering, be added unto either one of those these chastities, without any increase of fruitfulness. Next, when we set it down that many men and women so keep virginal chastity, as that yet they do not the things

which the Lord saith, "If thou wills to be perfect, go, sell all that thou hast, and give unto the poor, and thou shalt have treasure in Heaven: and come, follow me;" and dare not unite themselves to those dwelling together, among whom no one saith that anything is his own, but all things are unto them common; do we think that there is no addition of fruitfulness unto the virgins of God, when they do this? or that the virgins of God are without any fruit, although they do not this? Therefore there are many gifts, and some brighter and higher than others, each than each. And at times one is fruitful in fewer gifts, but better; another in lower gifts, but more. And in what manner they be either made equal one to another, or distinguished one from another, in receiving eternal honors, who of men would dare to pronounce? whereas yet it is plain both that those differences are many, and that the better are profitable not for the present time, but for eternity. But I judge that the Lord willed to make mention of three differences of fruitfulness, the rest He left to such as understand. For also another Evangelist hath made mention only of the hundred-fold: we are not, therefore, are we, to think that he either rejected, or knew not of, the other two, but rather that he left them to be understood?

47. But, as I had begun to say, whether the fruit an hundred-fold be virginity dedicated to God, or whether we are to understand that interval of fruitfulness in some other way, either such as we have made mention of, or such as we have not made mention of; yet no one, as I suppose, will have dared to prefer virginity to martyrdom, and no one will have doubted that this latter gift is hidden, if trial to test it be wanting. A virgin, therefore, hath a subject for thought, such as may be of profit to her for the

keeping of humility, that she violate not that charity, which is above all gifts, without which assuredly whatever other gifts she shall have had, whether few or many, whether great or small, she is nothing. She hath, I say, a subject for thought, that she be not puffed up, that she rival not; forsooth that she so make profession that the virginal good is much greater and better than the married good, as that yet she know not whether this or that married woman be not already able to suffer for Christ, but herself as yet unable, and she herein spared, that her weakness is not put to the question by trial. "For God," saith the Apostle, "is faithful, Who will not suffer you to be tried above what ye are able but will make with the trial a way out, that ye may be able to bear it." Perhaps, therefore, those men or women keeping a way of married life praiseworthy in its kind, are already able, against an enemy forcing to unrighteousness, to contend even by tearing in pieces of bowels, and shedding of blood; but these men or women, continent from childhood, and making themselves eunuchs for the sake of the Kingdom of Heaven, still are not as yet able to endure such, either for righteousness, or for chastity itself. For it is one thing, for truth and a holy purpose, not to consent unto one who would persuade and flatter, but another thing not to yield even to one who tortures and strikes. These lie hid in the powers and strength of souls, by trial they are unfolded, by actual essay they come forth. In order, therefore, that each be not puffed up by reason of that, which he sees clearly that he can do, let him humbly consider that he knows not that there is perchance something more excellent which he cannot do, but that some, who neither have nor profess that of which he is lawfully self-conscious, are able to do this, which he himself cannot do.

Thus will be kept, not by feigned but by true humility, "In honor preventing one another," and, "esteeming each the other higher than himself."

48. What now shall I say concerning the very carefulness and watchfulness against sin? "Who shall boast that he hath a chaste heart? or who shall boast that he is clean from sin?" Holy virginity is indeed inviolate from the mother's womb; but "no one," saith he, "is clean in Thy sight, not even the infant whose life is of one day upon the earth." There is kept also in faith inviolate a certain virginal chastity, whereby the Church is joined as a chaste virgin unto One Husband: but That One Husband hath taught, not only the faithful who are virgin in mind and body, but all Christians altogether, from spiritual even unto carnal, from Apostles even unto the last penitents, as though from the height of heaven even unto the bounds of it, to pray, and in the prayer itself hath admonished them to say, "And forgive us our debts, even as we also forgive our debtors:" where, by this which we seek, He shews what also we should remember that we are. For neither on behalf of those debts, which for our whole past life we trust have been forgiven unto us in Baptism through His peace, hath He charged us to pray, saying, "And forgive us our debts, even as we also forgive our debtors:" otherwise this were a prayer which Catechumens rather ought to pray up to the time of Baptism; but whereas it is what baptized persons pray, rulers and people, pastors and flocks; it is sufficiently shown that in this life, the whole of which is a trial, no one ought to boast himself as though free from all sins.

49. Wherefore also the virgins of God without blame indeed, "follow the Lamb whithersoever He shall have gone," both the cleansing of sins being perfected, and virginity being kept, which, were it lost, could not return: but, because that same Apocalypse itself, wherein such unto one such were revealed, in this also praises them, that "in their mouth there was not found a lie:" let them remember in this also to be true, that they dare not say that they have not sin. Forsooth the same John, who saw that, hath said this, "If we shall have said that we have not sin, we deceive our own selves, and the truth is not in us; but if we shall have confessed our faults, He is faithful and just, so as to forgive us our sins, and to cleanse us from all unrighteousness. But if we shall have said that we have not sinned, we shall make Him a liar, and His word shall not be in us." This surely is not said unto these or those, but unto all Christians, wherein virgins also ought to recognize themselves. For thus they shall be without a lie, such as in the Apocalypse they appeared. And by this means so long as there is not as yet perfection in heavenly height, confession in lowliness makes them without blame.

50. But, again, lest by occasion of this sentence, anyone should sin with deadly security, and should allow himself to be carried away, as though his sins were soon by easy confession to be blotted out, he straightway added, "My little children, these things have I written unto you, that ye sin not; and, if one shall have sinned, we have an Advocate with the Father, Jesus Christ the righteous, and Himself is a propitiation of our sins." Let no one therefore depart from sin as though about to return to it, nor bind himself as it were by compact of alliance of

this kind with unrighteousness, so as to take delight rather to confess it than to shun it. But, forasmuch as even upon such as are busy and on the watch not to sin, there creep by stealth, in a certain way, from human weakness, sins, however small, however few, yet not none; these same themselves become great and grievous, in case pride shall have added to them increase and weight: but by the Priest, Whom we have in the heavens, if by pious humility they be destroyed, they are with all ease cleansed.

51. But I contend not with those, who assert that a man can in this life live without any sin: I contend not, I gainsay not. For perhaps we take measure of the great from out our own misery, and, comparing ourselves with ourselves, understand not. One thing I know, that those great ones, such as we are not, such as we have not as yet made proof of, by how much they are great, by so much humble themselves in all things, that they may find grace before God. For, let them be how great so ever they will, "there is no servant greater than his Lord, nor disciple greater than his master." And assuredly He is the Lord, Who saith, "All things have been delivered unto Me of My Father;" and He is the Master, Who saith, "Come unto Me, all ye who labor, and learn of Me;" and yet what learn we? "In that I am meek," saith He, "and lowly of heart."

52. Here someone will say, This is now not to write of virginity, but of humility. As though truly it were any kind of virginity, and not that which is after God, which we had undertaken to set forth. And this good, by how much I see it to be great, by so much I fear for it, lest it be lost, the thief pride. Therefore there is none that

Of Holy Virginity

guarded the virginal good, save God Himself Who gave it: and God is Charity. The Guardian therefore of virginity is Charity: but the place of this Guardian is humility. There forsooth He dwelleth, Who said, that on the lowly and quiet, and that trembled at His words, His Spirit rested. What, therefore, have I done foreign from my purpose, if wishing the good, which I have praised, to be more securely guarded, I have taken care also to prepare a place for the Guardian? For I speak with confidence, nor have I any fear lest they be angry with me, whom I admonish with care to fear for themselves together with me. More easily do follow the Lamb, although not whithersoever He shall have gone, yet so far as they shall have had power, married persons who are humble, than virgins who are proud. For how doth one follow Him, unto Whom one wills not to approach or how doth one approach Him, unto Whom one comes not to learn, "in that I am meek and lowly of heart?" Wherefore those the Lamb leaded following whithersoever He shall have gone, in whom first Himself shall have found where to lay His Head. For also a certain proud and crafty person had said to Him, "Lord, I will follow Thee whithersoever Thou shalt have gone;" to whom He made answer, "Foxes have dens, and fowls of heaven nests: but the Son of Man hath not where to lay His Head." By the term of foxes, He reproved wily craftiness, and by the name of birds puffed-up arrogance, wherein He found not pious humility to rest in. And by this nowhere at all did he follow the Lord, who had promised that he would follow Him, not unto a certain point of progress, but altogether whithersoever He should have gone.

53. Wherefore this do ye, virgins of God, this do ye: follow ye the Lamb, whithersoever He shall have gone. But first come unto Him, Whom ye are to follow, and learn, in that He is meek and lowly of heart. Come ye in lowly wise unto the Lowly, if ye love: and depart not from Him, lest ye fall. For whoso fears to depart from Him asks and says, "Let there not come to me foot of pride." Go on in the way of loftiness with the foot of lowliness; Himself lifted up such as follow in lowly wise, Who thought it not a trouble to come down unto such as lay low. Commit ye His gifts unto Him to keep, "guard ye your strength unto Him." Whatever of evil through His guardianship ye commit not, account as forgiven unto you by Him: lest, thinking that you have little forgiven unto you, ye love little, and with ruinous boasting despise the publicans beating their breasts. Concealing that strength of yours which hath been tried beware, that ye be not puffed up, because ye have been able to bear something: but concerning that which hath been untried pray, that ye be not tempted above that ye are able to bear. Think that some are superior to you in secret, than whom ye are openly better. When the good things of others, haply unknown to you, are kindly believed by you, your own that are known to you are not lessened by comparison, but strengthened by love: and what haply as yet are wanting, are by so much the more easily given, by how much they are the more humbly desired. Let such among your number as persevere, afford to you an example: but let such as fall increase your fear. Love the one that ye may imitate it; mourn over the other, that ye be not puffed up. Do not ye establish your own righteousness; submit yourselves unto God Who justifies you. Pardon the sins of others, pray for your own: future sins shun by watching,

past sins blot out by confessing.

54. Lo, already ye are such, as that in the rest of your conduct also ye correspond with the virginity which ye have professed and kept. Lo, already not only do ye abstain from murders, devilish sacrifices and abominations, thefts, rapines, frauds, perjuries, drunkennesses, and all luxury and avarice, hatreds, emulations, impieties, cruelties; but even those things, which either are, or are thought, lighter, are not found nor arise among you: not bold face, not wandering eyes, not unbridled tongue, not petulant laugh, not scurrilous jest, not unbecoming mien, not swelling or loose gait; already ye render not evil for evil, nor curse for curse; already, lastly, ye fulfill that measure of love, that ye lay down your lives for your brethren. Lo, already ye are such, because also such ye ought to be. These, being added to virginity, set forth an angelic life unto men, and the ways of heaven unto the earth. But, by how much ye are great, whosoever of you are so great, "by so much humble yourselves in all things, that ye may find grace before God," that He resist you not as proud, that He humble you not as lifting up yourselves, that He lead you not through straits as being puffed up: although anxiety be unnecessary, that, where Charity glows, humility be not wanting.

55. If, therefore, ye despise marriages of sons of men, from which to beget sons of men, love ye with your whole heart Him, Who is fair of form above the sons of men; ye have leisure; your heart is free from marriage bonds. Gaze on the Beauty of your Lover: think of Him equal to the Father, made subject also to His Mother:

ruling even in the heavens, and serving upon the earth: creating all things, created among all things. That very thing, which in Him the proud mock at, gaze on, how fair it is: with inward eyes gaze on the wounds of Him hanging, the scars of Him rising again, the blood of Him dying, the price of him that believes, the gain of Him that redeems. Consider of how great value these are, weigh them in the scales of Charity; and whatever of love ye had to expend upon your marriages, pay back to Him.

56. It is well that He seeks your beauty within, where He hath given unto you power to become daughters of God: He seeks not of you a fair flesh, but fair conduct, whereby to bridle also the flesh. He is not one unto Whom anyone can lie concerning you, and make him rage through jealousy. See with how great security ye love Him, Whom ye fear not to offend by false suspicions. Husband and wife love each other, in that they see each other: and what they see not, that they fear between themselves: nor have they sure delight in what is visible, while in what is concealed they usually suspect what is not. Ye in Him, Whom ye see not with the eyes, and behold by faith, neither have what is real to blame, nor fear lest haply ye offend Him by what is false. If therefore ye should owe great love to husbands, Him, for Whose sake ye would not have husbands, how greatly ought ye to love? Let Him be fixed in your whole heart, Who for you was fixed on the Cross: let Him possess in your soul all that, whatever it be, that ye would not have occupied by marriage. It is not lawful for you to love little Him, for Whose sake ye have not loved even what were lawful. So loving Him Who is meek and lowly of heart, I have no fear for you of pride.

57. Thus, after our small measure, we have spoken enough both of sanctity, whereby ye are properly called "sanctimoniales," and of humility, whereby whatever great name ye bear is kept. But more worthily let those Three Children, unto whom He, Whom they loved with full glow of heart, afforded refreshing in the fire, admonish you concerning this our little work, much more shortly indeed in number of words, but much more greatly in weight of authority, in the Hymn wherein God is honored by them. For joining humility unto holiness in such as praise God, they have most plainly taught, that each, by how much he make any more holy profession, by so much do beware that he be not deceived by pride. Wherefore do ye also praise Him, Who grants unto you, that in the midst of the flames of this world, although ye be not joined in marriage, yet ye be not burned: and praying also for us, "Bless ye the Lord, ye holy and humble men of heart; utter a hymn, and exalt Him above all forever."

www.ingramcontent.com/pod-product-compliance
Lightning Source LLC
Chambersburg PA
CBHW052117070526
44584CB00017B/2526